A GHOST THRILLS AMERICA: True Account of A Haunting that Mesmerized A Nation

Dylan Clearfiel

IØ1Ø2273

Copyright © 2020 Prism Thomas

Second edition

G. Stempien Publishing Company

G. Stempien Publishing Company

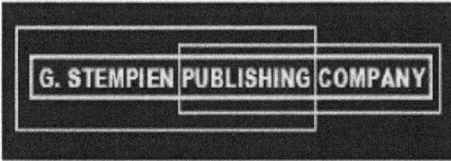

ISBN 978-0-930472-49-8

Editorial offices in New Quay, Cymru (Wales) UK.

CONTENTS

APPENDIX B

FRANCE IN ILLINOIS

APPENDIX C

A SMILAR GHOST STORY

INTRODUCTION

In 1932 an unearthly phenomenon occurred on property owned by the Illinois State Penitentiary at Joliet, Illinois. The voice of a singing ghost began to croon from the prison's potter's field. Instead of promoting the story or trying to study and understand the phenomenon the authorities tried to cover it up and brand it as nothing more than a hoax. They even provided the perpetrator.

This report re-opens the event of 1932 and produces newly uncovered evidence that explodes the hoax theory and proves that a real ghost was the cause of the haunting.

The story of the singing ghost was covered by local newspaper reporter Elmer Ott and others. Mr. Ott was extensively interviewed on this subject in 1982. Almost everyone believes that the reason for the silencing of the ghost is that the hoax was uncovered and the perpetrator was revealed. This will be proved to be incorrect.

The singing ghost was explained away as having been a trustee assigned to the prison quarry during the night and his singing was heard by people far and wide. Promotion of this false story by the local newspapers is probably why an event that in its time had had national coverage was eventually forgotten.

Among the information that will be produced in this report are facts which demonstrate how the hoax theory was not only misleading but it was a physical impossibility. The phenomenon of the singing ghost simply could not have happened as the authorities described.

I was raised and lived in the neighborhood where the haunting took place and the specific locations where all of the events happened are extremely well known to me. In fact, there probably isn't another person living or passed on who had equal or more intimate knowledge than myself of the layout and the physical terrain of the Prison Field where it all happened. This is critical knowledge to possess when solving the mystery of the singing ghost because so much of it deals with the distances and the terrain involved.

I could no longer let the trustee-as-singing-ghost-theory go unchallenged. It was a part of my own local folklore and history that had been distorted and the time came to correct the error. I decided to investigate the event more deeply and, through information supplied by the contemporary newspapers and first-hand witnesses, discovered the real truth behind the singing ghost. I briefly covered this story in a section of a previous book called *"Chicagoland Ghosts"* but have since decided that a much fuller coverage was needed as new facts emerged.

While re-examining the history of this case I discovered astounding new evidence. Indisputable evidence. Physical evidence! A picture of the ghost who may have done the haunting was raised from a decades old photo album!

The singing ghost of Joliet prison was not a hoax. The voice that drew thousands upon thousands of people into a dark, marshy field in the depths of the morning hours came from a genuine spirit. And he had been captured on film and was only waiting to be discovered.

CHAPTER ONE – WHERE IT HAPPENED

In 1932, as now, the city of Joliet was divided into an East Side and a West Side by the Des Plaines River.

However, then but not maybe so much now, the two sides of town were also separated economically as well. The wealthy people lived on the West Side and the economically challenged people lived on the East Side. My parents and I lived on the East Side.

The famous hauntings that are the subject of this book – there are two hauntings in reality – took place on the East Side of the city. One haunting was on the 700 acre property owned by the Illinois State Penitentiary and the other was in a nearby subdivision.

Two of the most strategic streets in Joliet were then Collins Street and Woodruff Road. Woodruff Road intersects Collins Street at what has become the main administrative building of the Old prison.

It has been shown on television many times, particularly in the making of the Early Edition program with Kyle Chandler.

Collins Street was the most direct route from Joliet to Chicago and was the road that most of the traffic from up north followed to get to Joliet. Anyone who has seen the movie "Blues Brothers" has seen Collins Street because it is the street up which Dan Akroyd drove "Joliet Jake" after his release from the real Joliet Prison.

That scene was totally accurate. Below is a photo of the east side exit from the prison itself as used in the movie.

The Prison Field consists of a lower field and another field, which looks like a plateau, on top of it. It is on this upper field where the potter's burial ground is located and from where the ghost did its singing. However, the spirit also appeared to frightened witnesses on the lower field as well.

In 1932 an extensive barbed wire fence was strung all along the Prison Field borders, containing the 700 acre area (about the size of 7 football fields). At the time, cows used the lower field for grazing. In the center of the field was a pond that disappeared in the dry season.

Below is a photograph of the Prison Field taken as it looked in 1932 from Edgehill Street which bordered the field directly to the east. Shown is about half of the field's total area. The field extends much farther to the left and there is a very high, steep hill on the right.

Potter's field is located on the upper field near the front of the hilltop. Unclaimed prisoners who'd died for various reasons while incarcerated were buried here. Their graves were marked only by small concrete slabs. Most of the slabs were placed level with the ground, but a few stood upright. This was the most sought after ground by ghost hunters during the height of the haunting. Many people literally sat on the graves, hoping for a closer contact with the spirit.

Beyond the potter's field is a vast empty plain that stretches about a half mile to the extreme northern edge and the neighboring town of Lockport. There is a deep, narrow chasm in the center of this wide expanse whose walls and floor contain a treasure of fossils of ancient life in the area. Descending into this chasm is like going backwards millions of years into the past. The silence is overwhelming. Once in the bottom of the ravine a person cannot hear any sounds from beyond it.

Such is the basic layout of the entire area which the singing ghost haunted during the second half of the month of July in 1932.

CHAPTER TWO – THE SINGING BEGINS

The year is 1932. Joliet is a steel town of about 45,000 people which is wallowing deep in the Great Depression. Thousands of jobs had been lost and the homes of this conservative Midwestern town are suffering from the ravages of unemployment.

In world news during July 1932, Hitler was continuing his buildup toward war while at the same time diplomats were meeting with German officials in Lausanne where it was agree to wipe out the remainder of that country's payments of reparations for World War I. Also in April 1932, Japan marched into Manchuria and Austria was paid a huge sum not to enter into a political and economic union with Germany.

But in the United States the Depression was still the average citizen's major concern. Without jobs to go to, people had a lot of time on their hands. Especially in the evenings and late at night. During the day a person might seek non-existent jobs or scrounge for extra food for the family.

But when night came people would linger on their front porches in the summer and then retire inside to listen to the radio. If the night was particularly hot and humid people would return outdoors to their porches after the radio went off the air in search of any cool air they could find.

The night of July 15, 1932 was a hot and sultry one. Many people had escaped to their porches after turning off the radio. If you lived on Edgehill Street, which directly bordered the vast 700 acre field owned by the Illinois State Penitentiary, the only sounds to be heard were the crickets and frogs.

Except this night. Just as the full moon made its appearance, a new and strange sound was heard floating through the neighborhood. Below is a photo from the 1990's of Edgehill Street looking northward.

Singing was coming from somewhere. The first explanation that occurred to account for it was that one of the neighbors had his radio turned up too loud. But at this time of night radio generally had stopped broadcasting for the day. But also, the type of singing didn't sound like the type of music that usually came from the radio. It sounded like the hymns sung at church.

The first person officially to hear the singing was the mother of a man named Stanley Dudek. The back yard of their house on Juniper Street - which was on the top of the hill - bordered the barbed wire fence of the potter's field. Mrs. Dudek was drawn to her backyard at

11:30 pm on the night of July 15th by the ghostly voice as noted by her 21 year-old son. (Some say the singing actually began after midnight on the 16th).

"My mother heard the singing first of all," said Stanley in an interview with the *Joliet Evening-Herald.* *"She was in the house with my sister Genevieve the Saturday before last and heard the singing about 11:30 o'clock. They went out in the back to see who was*

singing and turned flashlights on the spot, but could see no one. My father, George Dudek, and I were out that night, but heard the singing the next night and went out into the cemetery to investigate. We found nothing. Other neighbors have also heard the voice.

"We heard it every night until the crowds began to bother the "thing." It has a sweet voice, but very strong, all the words can never be distinguished. We think it sings in Latin. Starting with low, hideous, gurgling sounds, the song breaks suddenly strong and reaches very high notes. But it is a beautiful singer."

Stanley Dudek then finished, saying, *"If they catch the one singing they ought to put him on the stage, ghost or not."*

That's how the haunting began. Over the next several days, the singing came nightly, starting between

11:30 and midnight. The news rapidly spread from neighborhood to neighborhood, and the regular gathering of listeners assembled in the Prison Field to hear the voice of a singing ghost.

The first people to hear the singing coming from Potter's field lived on Juniper Street. The alleged hoaxer was supposedly perpetrating his hoax from the quarry at the bottom of a 700 foot high hill. The quarry is almost a mile distant from Juniper Street.

In 1932, the Penitentiary authorities understood this problem and addressed it. Their finding was that the limestone walls of the quarry provided a type of amplification. They argued that the quarry walls acted as "sounding boards" for their chosen hoaxer and transmitted his voice across vast distances, making it appear to come from a different location. They compared it to a ventriloquist throwing his voice, making it seem to come from another source. And that was where they made their first tactical mistake.

When this explanation was offered, a local newspaper did interviews with professional ventriloquists and their response was that the quarry-as-sounding-board theory was nonsense. Not only would the intervening hill BLOCK the passage of any sound from below, but the sound of the singing would be trapped within the limestone walls of the quarry not be amplified by them.

The ventriloquists added further that the primary feature of ventriloquism was something called misdirection. The idea was to misdirect the hearer so that he thinks the sound is coming from somewhere else. This obviously was impossible in the case of the singing ghost. No one really had any idea where the sound was coming from and so no one could not be misdirected from a location he did not know existed.

And as such, the explanation of the prison officials was a different form of misdirection, attempting to lead the public into believing something that did not make any logical sense. Likewise, it too failed.

It's important to note that the singing was heard all throughout the neighborhoods, including at the bottom of the Prison Field hill. This totally defeats the sounding board theory because this would imply that the singing from the quarry went in two directions at the same time, first up the hill to the grave sites then down the hill to the neighborhood streets. How plausible is that?

I am intimately familiar with this hill and the entire area. It was my childhood playground. The slope from the quarry to the top of the hill is quite steep. The face of the hill itself is also a steep climb. In addition to this, there are shallow caves scattered throughout the hillside along with occasional ravines. And during the day a large herd of cows was pastured in the mucky field below and was attended by a pair of rifle bearing guards. These facts will be significant later.

It was not an easy hike for any of the people who trekked through the field itself to get to the old graveyard. Not only was it a rugged, steep hike up the slope but the ground leading up to it was marshy and punctured with cow prints. There was another, easier route to take and that was up the inclined Edgehill Street directly past my house. This led almost directly to the potter's field. A photo of contemporary 1932 Edgehill Street below.

My parents told me of the throngs of people who marched past their house during that exciting July of 1932. At first, it was only neighborhood people going by, but later the crowds were greatly swelled by sightseers from all over the country. It must have been pretty confusing for these foreigners to find themselves trudging up a dark gravel road into the night not quite sure where they were being led.

My parents (above) heard the ghost, too, of course. But they heard it coming from the field outside the back yard of where they lived on Edgehill Street. This was well below the potter's field and about quarter of a mile from the base of hill. Might this be a roaming ghost?

GHOST THRILLS HUNDREDS AT POTTERS' FIELD

Crowds Wait All Night for Eerie Song at Graves of Convicts.

At first the atmosphere surrounding the singing ghost was solemn and respectful. This was a ghost who was singing church hymns in what sounded like Latin. What could be holier than that?

During the first few days of the ghost's appearance it was a neighborhood phenomenon. Most of the visitors to the Prison Field walked to the area with subdued voices and in an orderly march.

Not everyone was convinced that the ghost was real. In fact, during the first week many attempts were made to flush out whoever was perpetrating the hoax. Gangs of youths got together with torches and flashlights sweeping the fields and hills in search of anyone who might've been faking the singing. No one was ever found.

The scapegoat who'd later been named as the hoaxer – a prisoner named William Lalon Chrysler – when asked about the people searching for him said that he would simply hide behind a bush when he heard them coming. This is absurd. First of all, there aren't any bushes large enough to hide behind in a quarry. A limestone quarry consists of walls and ground of pure limestone. Second, if he were inside the quarry he would have been hopelessly trapped by any hunters. There was no exit from the quarry except through the front. I know this because I visited this quarry often.

Remember, the supposed hoaxer was a prisoner. Transferred from Cook County Jail, W.L. Chrysler was serving time for grand larceny and was due to be released in three weeks. And as a prisoner – even though a trustee – he had to have been under guard. If he were hiding from search parties he couldn't simply run off to wherever he chose.

This brings up a question that no one seems to have asked: why didn't any of the search parties find him or why didn't a guard report on his crooning activities? Chrysler theoretically was assigned to man the sump pumps in the quarry. Why didn't someone simply march to the noisily operating sump pumps if for no other reason than to see what all the commotion was about? Maybe the sump pumps weren't even in operation! The quarry was thoroughly searched more than once. No one was ever there. It appears that the man suspected of being the hoaxer wasn't even where the authorities claimed he was.

And suppose Chrysler was in the quarry hiding behind a bush as he'd claimed. How did he find his way around in the pitch dark? He had to have had some kind of light with him. In the pitch dark of a quarry even the tiniest light would glow as a beacon, even a simple match light. How could this light possibly not have been seen by searchers?

Below is a picture of the quarry near the Joliet Penitentiary taken around the period in question. Notice the series of railroad tracks that lead into the quarry. These are extending from the main line of the EJ&E

Railroad, giving a better indication of precisely where the quarry was located.

Another location that received close searching was the graveyard itself. Clearly, no one could have been hiding anywhere in this area of flat ground. There wasn't any place to hide.

But was it possible that one or more of the grave markers had been wired for sound? Had someone connected a speaker to it from which the ghostly singing could have been coming? The answer is no.

Every rock, bush and headstone was examined both at night and in the daylight with nothing suspicious being found. Word spread rapidly that there was a real ghost to be heard in Joliet's Prison Field. People began to stream to the area from all over the country.

CHAPTER FOUR – BEFORE THE SIGHTSEERS

Before the sightseers came, the mood was a friendly one where neighbors sat together among the grave stones and counted down the minutes toward midnight when the ghost traditionally started singing. It was like a community picnic. Families came with children, even at this late hour. People brought thermoses of hot – or cold – beverages, blankets and flashlights.

A description of the scene from one of the local newspapers:

Six hundred persons visited the scene last night, coming after nine o'clock and many staying thru the night.

In the cemetery youths and adults stumble over sunken graves and trip over head-stones in the dark bold youths form patrols and with torchlights and lanterns inspect every square foot of the cemetery, looking for hidden wires which may prove the Singing Spectre a hoax. But in ten nights, now, none have been found.

As midnight approaches silence settles down and many lights are dimmed. Only low conversation is heard, where before all was hubbub. Midnight is the hour when all union ghosts do their stuff, it is remembered.

Story-tellers collect groups and thrill their listeners with ghost stories, and, perhaps, even recall their own with ghosts. Others stimulate themselves with the thought that no such things are real.

"But this one is real," a voice says out of the darkness, "I heard it myself last night —"

"So did I, it was only five feet behind me —"

If left alone the voice goes on several minutes, but daring boys with lanterns usually ferret out the spot and the singing stops.

That last observation was critical. The voice was real; it was coming from a specific location. And when it was tracked down – it stopped. How is it possible that a man who is singing in a quarry about a half mile away at the bottom of a vast hill could know in 1932 that a group of boys had located the spot where the voice was being heard and evade them without notice? It is a physical impossibility. No one had special electronic eavesdropping devices in these days.

During the first days of the haunting, people from the extended neighborhoods in Joliet, Lockport, Crest Hill and Rockdale drove to the Prison Field and parked on prison land. Obliging youths at this time directed traffic down Woodruff Road and into the field.

As noted in the newspaper article as many as 600 people at a time showed up in these early days and most of them made the trek up the high hill from their parked cars. Once atop the hill they joined the crowd already gathered around the graves.

Below is a contemporary photo taken of a group of people keeping close watch of a grave in Potter's field (courtesy *Joliet Spectator*).

The ghost made a very special appearance one day around dusk. It was before any of even the earliest arrivals had shown up for their nightly vigil. A fisherman was making his way home from the pond through the Prison Field after a day of fishing. As he continued along, a voice from behind asked him, "Any luck tonight?"

The fisherman turned around to reply but there wasn't anyone there. It was the ghost. In an interview with the local newspaper, this is the internal conversation the fisherman said he was having with himself, *"I had little if any luck fishing. And if I don't have any better running than I did fishing I don't know what I'm going to do."*

According to the rest of the story, he didn't fare very well running, either. En route across the field he got a foot snagged in one of the deep cow prints in the turf and slammed to the ground. He claimed that the momentum of his tumble caused him to roll the rest of the way to Woodruff Road.

This is a critical piece of evidence for many reasons. It proved that the ghost was not tied to one spot and that it did travel from the cemetery area. Also of extreme importance: **THE GHOST WAS HEARD AT A TIME WHEN THE ALLEGED HOAXER COULD NOT HAVE BEEN IN THE QUARRY!** In addition to this, the only place in the Prison Field where the man could have been fishing was in the small pond that was near the quarry! He surely would have spotted the convict if he had been in the quarry.

But there's more. Judging by the description of where the fisherman had encountered the ghost and how far he had to run to get to Woodruff Road (100 yards would have been the calculated distance) it is clear that he saw the spirit somewhere off my parents' back yard. Why is this important? Because it is roughly at this location where a picture of the ghost was taken. And it wasn't discovered until about 80 years later!

The information supplied by this encounter with the ghost is in itself enough to exorcise the hoax theory. Ironically, no one has ever seen this phantom trustee manning the sump pumps in the quarry but thousands have heard the singing ghost. Doesn't it seem more likely that the convict trustee is more of a hoax than the ghost?

SINGING GHOST FAILS TO APPEAR BEFORE 3000

"Too Much Noise and Excitement," Say Those Who Have Heard It.

THRONGS WAIT

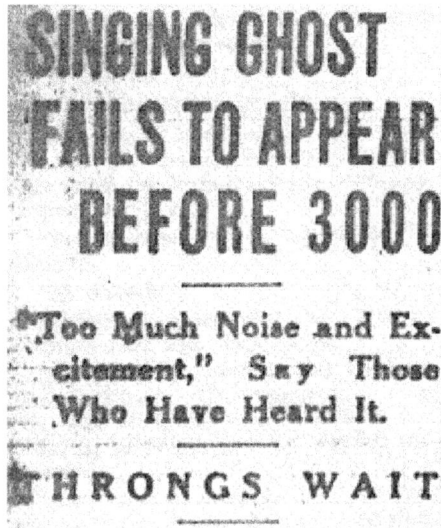

After the first ten days, news of the singing ghost had spanned the nation. People were driving to the Prison Field from all across the country. Driving distances of 25 miles or more was a very difficult proposition in 1932. The national highway system wouldn't be constructed for another thirty years.

Most roads weren't paved and consisted of gravel or simply dirt paths. The country roads that did exist were like labyrinths, and maps – when they could be found – couldn't possibly accurately pinpoint all of the roads. And filling stations were not nearly as available as they are today. Thus, for someone to drive to Joliet from anywhere out of state would have been a major undertaking.

A person named Joshua Jones from Sickle Center, Missouri was one of those out-of-staters who endured the long drive and camped out at the Prison Field graveyard. According to him:

"Folks in my town read of this Singing Spectre in the newspaper but they won't believe it until they hear from me, and you have to show me."

From nearby, a man with an Irish accent offered, *"Sure, and it may be the banshee crying. Back in the days when I lived in the auld country, I heard her often. She crys(sic) steadily, night after night, when some good soul dies on earth. Perhaps her Gaelic has been mistaken for Latin. She is a little old woman, and always combing and brushing her streaming gray hair as she cries."*

So, this man heard the voice singing in Gaelic rather than Latin. The only things about the voice of the singing ghost that are agreed upon by all is that it is loud and strong and it isn't in English. None of the witnesses understood any of the words.

With the arrival of the outsiders the atmosphere changed and the haunting pattern of the ghost also changed. Instead of singing around midnight as usual the ghost delayed his performances until much later in the morning, after the faithless had become frustrated and left the area. At least, that's what the local people believed.

"He doesn't like crowds," those familiar with the ghost declared, noted the author of the *Joliet Evening-Herald* article. *"It has made him obstinate to see these people stomping about the graves and disturbing his thoughts and the thoughts of his mates.*

"Last night came and went with no spirit singing. The ghost sings only when the crowd is quiet and still, the regulars claim. The first night it gave its eerie call at

11:45 o'clock, and one night it sang at midnight sharp, but it is usually later than that. The crowd, in the majority, is content to sit and wait. Sunday the Latin songs came from nowhere at 4 o'clock in the morning.

"Those who stayed up that late say they heard the singing at 3 o'clock this morning, after the rowdy unbelieving persons had left for home."

The article continued: *Retiring in the face of superior odds, the Singing Spectre moped in his convict's grave in Potter's field . . . when 3000 noisy persons appeared to hear the Latin song he has sung, it is said, for ten consecutive nights.*

"The ghost is self-conscious," the believers say, "and doesn't like to be laughed at. . ."

There was even more trouble with the coming of the "outsiders." They had attracted an unwanted element to the site of the haunting. Groups of young thugs had appeared and started charging people to park their cars in the Prison Field. The charge was 15 cents to enter and another 15 cents upon leaving. If the fee was not paid, the car owner's windshield would be broken.

The authorities now took notice. Not only had an illegal car parking ring developed, but people who lived in the area were having their property vandalized and they themselves were being threatened. In addition to this, full scale trespassing was taking place on prison grounds and damage had already been done to the barbed wire fence which had been stamped into the earth in many spots. Even the herd of cows was now being affected, having to be kept inside while all of this was taking place. Something had to be done to bring an end to the singing ghost problem.

Now that the ghost had seemingly stopped singing for some reason the authorities needed to furnish an explanation for the phenomenon. This was when they revised their initial story about the convict singing in the quarry. The authorities probably felt that if they could discredit the ghost – and if he co-operated by not singing for a couple of nights in a row – they could peacefully remove the crowds from prison property and keep them away before the singing resumed if it did. By that time, they would have regained control of the situation and would be able to keep any future crowds at a distance.

Most people don't know that the authorities had another explanation at the ready to use to discount the singing ghost. It may even have been considered prior to the first story about the convict's voice carrying from the quarry but wasn't used until later. I don't believe the second story was ever widely publicized.

The second explanation for the ghost was that it was a convict who was in an underground bunker where he sang Masses in Latin to himself. The sound of his singing was carried to the surface by a ventilation pipe.

This was the story that I was told by my parents and by other people of the neighborhood.

However, the same problem hampered this story: no one was ever able to find the underground bunker. When a child, I spent a great deal of time looking for it throughout the Prison Field. Of course, it's difficult to find something that never existed.

This alternative explanation removes any semblance of credibility to the authorities. There wasn't any truth behind either explanation of the singing ghost. They were just stories to defuse the situation.

CHAPTER SIX – THE OTHER HAUNTINGS

As noted earlier, there was another haunting taking place at roughly the same time in roughly the same area as that of the singing ghost. The 2 hauntings have since been confused with each other. The other "haunting" occurred in a house in "The Hill" subdivision and was quickly exposed of as a hoax. Since this ghost story was confused with the singing ghost event this may be one other reason why so many people have classed the singing ghost as a hoax. They simply mistake the two as the same.

There isn't any information available on the specifics of "The Hill" haunting. However, I have two indisputable sources about the event. One of them is Elmer Ott who covered the story for the *Joliet Spectator Newspaper*. And the other source is my father, who would only divulge the fact of the haunting and little more. The "haunting" had occurred in his youth and he remembered few of the details and chose to keep the rest a mystery.

My father is a primary source because he was one of the main engineers of this haunting on "The Hill". At the time of the haunting my father was a freshman at Joliet Township High and had a reputation as a prankster and troublemaker. None of his activity was illegal or destructive, just irritating. Many people believe that I inherited this ability to be irritating from him.

At any rate, my father was the instigator of the faked haunting of the house on "The Hill". That is how he acquired his lifelong nickname – Jitter. It was because he was proficient at giving people the jitters.

In later years, there occurred another legitimate haunting in proximity to the Prison Field where the ghost sang. This location was in the house directly next door to my parent's house on Edgehill Street.

I covered this story as well in my earlier book *"Chicagoland Ghosts."* The section was called THE WITCH"S KNOCK. The haunting took place in the early 1960's and concerned the after effects of the sudden death of the woman who owned the house next to ours who was suspected of being a witch.

The woman's name was Mrs. Sable and she lived alone in her two story house on a large property that was in the shape of an isosceles triangle that came to an extreme point near the prison's Potter's field. Her old dark house and her expansive yard were hidden under great amounts of foliage which seemed to keep the property under shade even in the winter time. Walnut, pear, cherry, apple and other fruit and nut trees grew in abundance. Wild herbs and other plants of all shape and type filled her yard to the rim, being of such a vast variety that her yard might well have been a botanical garden.

These were just the type of exotic plants that a witch would use in working up her magical brews. The land even had its own water well accessed by an old-fashioned hand pump. And Mrs. Sable was rarely seen!

WAS THIS WOMAN REALLY A WITCH?

One day, Mrs. Sable died. No one knew it. Few people ever saw her, she never had any visitors and she lived all alone. Eventually, she was found dead, lying inches from her front door, reaching for it with her cane. The body was whisked off with such secrecy and speed it seemed as if the Devil had swept her away.

The Sable house remained empty after her death. Most of the furniture was removed from the upstairs, but the downstairs remained filled with crockery, plates, and mason jars. It was a very spooky place.

The house stayed dormant for many years, slowly falling into ruin while the vegetation grew rampant around it. Then one sunny summer afternoon several years after the death of Mrs. Sable something very extraordinary happened and I was witness to it. A loud, unearthly rapping came from the house. It was a brief series of knocks as if someone was striking a wooden door with a wooden cane. But the volume of the sound was far louder than a normal knock; it filled the neighborhood, and well beyond.

I immediately rushed to the Sable house in search of whoever was making the knocking sound. No one was there. And no one had been there. If someone had fled the property I would have certainly heard him rushing off through the vegetation filled yard. After doing a thorough search of the house and finding no one there, I returned to my yard nearby and scratched my head with wonder. Where had that noise come from?

Then I received another surprise. A friend from another neighborhood about half a mile away appeared at the front gate of my yard.

"I came over to see what all that knocking was about," he said.

"You heard that all the way over at your place?" I asked.

He then realized how odd that would be, to hear such a sound from so far away. Below is a map to show the distance involved.

Many years afterwards, I received more confirmation from others who'd read my book *"Chicagoland Ghosts"* that they too had heard this supernatural knock.

This ghostly knocking was the only supernatural phenomenon I ever knew to have originated from Mrs. Sable's house. My explanation for it is that it was an ethereal replay of the fallen woman's desperate knocking on her door with her cane for help in the last moments of her earthly existence. This time, someone heard it. Unfortunately, it was too late to help her unless she'd been calling for someone to pray for her restless soul.

There are two things significant about this haunting. One is that it demonstrates the presence of a psychic atmosphere in this area which is conducive to spiritual manifestations. And, second, sound seems to be the primary medium for contacting the other side here. But not just that. Sound seems also to be magnified in this area by an almost supernatural means. And this will be demonstrated time and time again.

FIND GHOST IS ONLY CONVICT SINGING AT WORK

Trusty Who Inspected Pumps in Quarry Croons Ballads During Night.

SOME UNCONVINCED

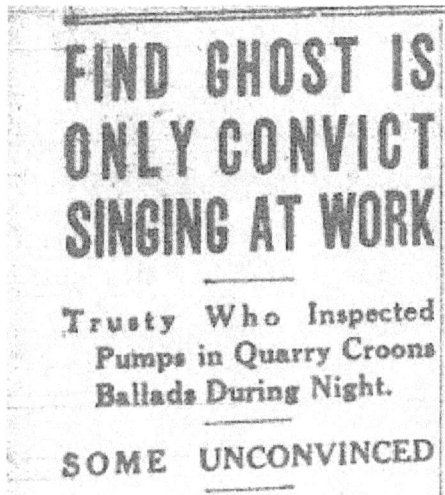

The authorities would have us believe that the reason that the ghost stopped singing was because the man who was perpetrating the hoax had learned of the commotion he was causing and stopped before he got into real trouble. Fourteen days after the fact!

Search parties were sent out after the ghost starting on the second night of the singing. The entire Prison Field was combed, including the quarry. Can anyone believe that the supposed hoaxer didn't see any of these search parties - especially the ones that ventured into his quarry? He himself admitted that he'd hide behind a bush when people came looking for him. Who did he think he was hiding from - casual hikers?

Even at the beginning of the haunting hundreds of people came to the Prison Field to hear the ghost. Can anyone believe that he didn't hear any of the commotion caused by hundreds of people in the otherwise silent darkness? He didn't notice all of the cars being parked in the middle of the Prison Field?

The authorities were asking the citizenry to believe that the voice of a lone man sitting in the midst of quarry could be heard singing above the constant drone of an industrial strength sump pump while at the same time this man could not hear the sounds being made by hundreds of trespassers on prison property?

The sump pump adds another problem to the hoax theory. How could a man's singing be heard over a sump pump? As important as this: how could a man's voice be heard over an operating sump pump when the sound of the sump pump couldn't be heard by anyone?

Why didn't a single person report hearing a sump pump in operation! The absurdities continue to mount.

Also consider the matter from the convict's point of view. He was due to be paroled in three weeks. Would he want to do anything to jeopardize that? Creating a full scale incident by pretending to be a ghost while on property owned by the state penitentiary would not seem to be a very good idea.

Why did William Lalon Chrysler admit to being the creator of the ghostly singing, claiming that he was chanting Irish folk songs because doing so comforted him? The reason he admitted to perpetrating a hoax is because that is what the authorities told him to do. They needed a scapegoat and he needed to keep his parole intact.

It is quite clear that the singing ghost was not simply a convict singing in a quarry. The facts make this explanation impossible. If that is the case, though, why did the singing stop and who was actually doing it?

Among all of the activities that were taking place at the Potter's field was one which barely anyone took notice of – a séance-exorcism. In a discrete ceremony before the sightseers arrived for the night a group of psychics gathered at the grave site and performed the ritual, both contacting a ghost and cleansing the ground. The hope was to help the soul or souls of any anguished spirits in the potter's field to move on to the next world. Very few people knew of this ceremony and it didn't receive newspaper coverage. Apparently the ceremony was successful.

Unfortunately, the outcome is all that is known about the ritual. Neither the identity of the spirit nor its reason for the haunting were discovered then. But there is some very convincing evidence now, including a photograph of the spirit taken many years after the fact.

STELLA VOLAN AND EVELYN BOJT TELL SHERIFF OLIVER FLINT AT GRAVE SITE ABOUT THEIR EXPERIENCES WITH THE SINGING GHOST (courtesy *The Joliet Spectator*)

CHAPTER EIGHT – SEEING A GHOST

I did not take the photograph you are about to see. I don't know who did take it. It must have been taken by someone in my family because it was in my possession along with all of the other old family photographs.

I came upon this picture while looking for a photograph that showed a view of my former back yard and a glimpse of the Prison Field beyond it. I had no idea that there was anything as significant in this photograph as what I discovered.

How odd is it that I – a ghost hunter for four decades – had in my possession a picture of a ghost and had no idea it even existed? When first looking at this photograph it seems totally ordinary. There seemed nothing unusual about it.

But when I scanned the picture into my computer system and in the process enlarged and magnified the background I quickly discovered that this was far from an ordinary photograph. There was something there that I'd never noticed before. A ghost! And it had always been there. Even without the magnification the ghost can be seen if a person looks in the right location.

The implications became immediately obvious. The photograph was taken around the period when the singing ghost was active and the visual anomaly was placed in a location where it would be expected to be. This is why the episode with the fisherman who spoke to the ghost was so important. It happened near the spot where the ghost in the photograph is standing.

The ghost is standing directly beneath the arrow.

In addition to the ghost, a manifestation of detached ectoplasm, or numerous orbs, were also caught on film. Note the 2 bright spots inside the sheds behind the boys in the photograph.

Below is a closeup.

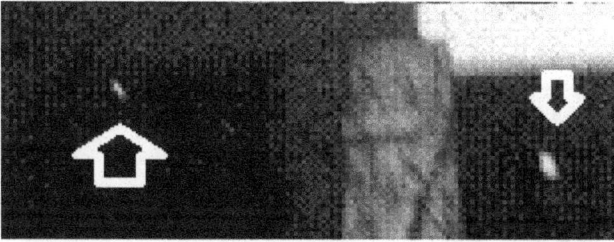

But when examining the entire photograph, a great many smaller pieces of ectoplasm can also be seen all about the entire area. (note circles in photo).

The actual figure of the ghost itself is on the right side of the photograph from the viewer's perspective. It is standing in what had been my old back yard and is as if it is watching the children.

Is the apparition that the arrow is pointing to the famous singing ghost?

The fence by which he is standing was an uncommonly tall one, being almost six feet in height. This would measure the ghostly figure at a height of about 5' 10". Directly behind the spirit is the Prison Field.

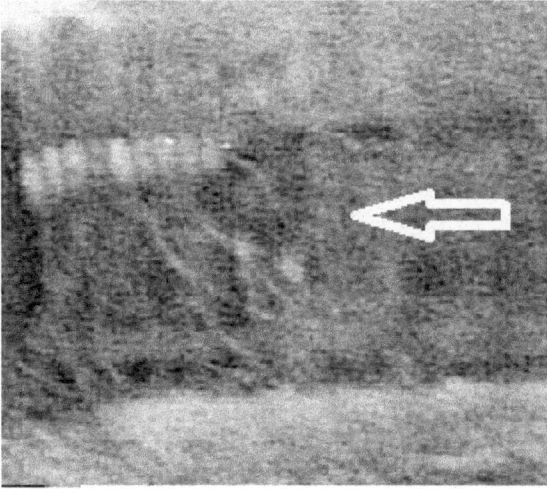

One matter was of serious concern when the photo of the ghost was first examined in close up. Why was its right arm bent at such a sharp angle? Under closer magnification it became obviously clear that a mass of ectoplasm was enveloping – hiding – the right shoulder making the right arm seem to be bent oddly.

Ectoplasm is a significant phenomenon in its own right and deserves a close examination since there is so much of it visible in these photographs. The type of ectoplasm seen in these photos is that which is exuded by a ghost and can be either an example of partial materialization or else extraneous material belonging to a spirit that is already mostly materialized. It is in a sense a material representation of energy.

The term ectoplasm was created by the French Nobel Prize winner Professor Charles Richet in the late 19th century. Ectoplasm is a combination of the Greek words ecto (exteriorized) and plasma (substance) and although not much used today it is still a useful description.

According to Professor Richet, who worked as a physiologist at the Sorbonne in Paris, ectoplasm passed through three stages. In the first stage it was invisible under normal light but could be photographed with infrared film and that it could be weighed. In its secondary stage it can be either vaporous, liquid, or solid and is accompanied by an ozone like odor.

In its third stage ectoplasm can be seen and felt and has the consistency of cobwebs. Further study by Professor Richet demonstrated that a third stage ectoplasm can weigh a mere few ounces to a more significant number ranging around twenty pounds. Ectoplasm seems to exist in a temperature zone of around 40 degrees Fahrenheit.

The ectoplasm in the photograph below is an unusually large amount of the substance. It is possible that it represents the energy of several ghosts in the process of attempting to materialize as well as being an extension of the one spirit that is already in view.

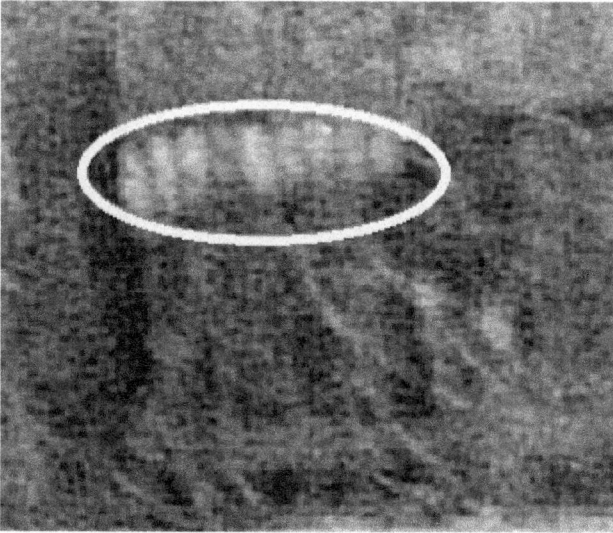

The many instances of ectoplasm scattered throughout the photograph may be residue energy rather than independent spirits.

Next examine the lower half of the ghost. Notice where his legs are in relation to the bottom crosspiece of the fence, or that long piece of wood which stabilizes the individual pickets. If you look close enough you can even be able to make out the footgear he's wearing.

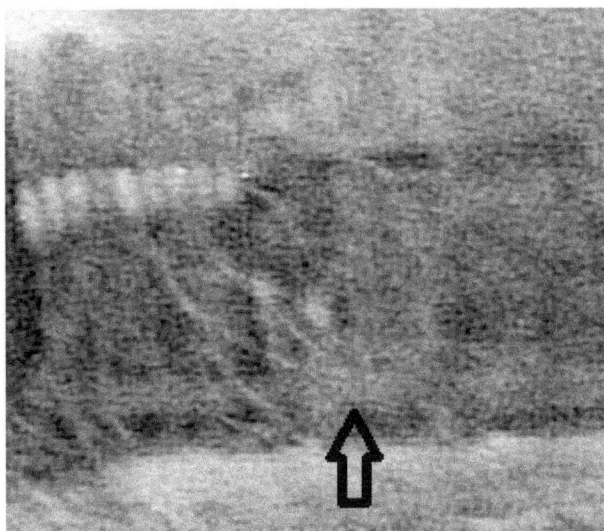

The crosspiece (arrow) extends in front of his legs at the shin level. His lower portion is behind the fence. Now look at his upper half. It is clearly standing in front of the fence. The upper crosspiece is behind the figure. But the ectoplasm is behind the fence like the figure's shins and lower legs. Oddly, his feet jut out on the near side of the fence below the crosspiece and as such are also in front of the fence.

This interweaving of form in and out of the fence is critically important. First it rules out the possibility that this is somehow a picture of a real person. No one could stand interwoven between a fence like that.

Second it rules out a double exposure. Similarly, a living person who was photographed would have to have been on one side of the fence or the other, not both sides at once. And another possibility that is ruled out is that of a hoax. A person would have to be a master photographic technician to create a picture of this nature. Although, I don't even know if it is possible.

Some people might claim that this isn't really a photograph of a human figure but simply an optical illusion. However, for this to simply be an optical illusion that would imply that a host of humanlike features would have randomly appeared on a photograph at the exact locations and in the exact proportions that would be required to produce the form of a person.

For example, the head on the body in this photo is where a head on a normal person would be expected to be – above the middle of the shoulders. Likewise the positioning of the arms, torso, hips, legs, feet and – most particularly – the hands.

Focus on the hands. They are being held in a palms outward position with the fingers – 5 of them – spread wide apart. It's as if the person in the picture had his hands raised in fear, attempting to fend off an attack of some type, maybe even a gunshot.

Below are the hands in the photograph. Count the fingers which are where they would be expected to be and of the right size as well.

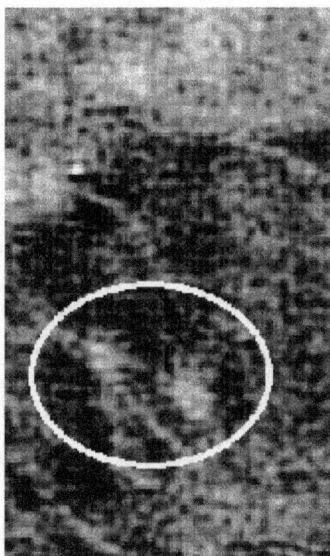

The hands are in the circle. This is the highest magnification possible. The fingers on the figure's right hand are more difficult to see but they are curved. His left hand is relatively sharp. Remember, in the original photograph the apparition was about 100 feet in the distance and this view of the hands is under extreme magnification.

Some observers may claim that it is simply a trick of light and shadow that only looks like hands. That would make it another very odd coincidence in a number of odd coincidences that are adding up. What are the odds that a trick of light and shadow combine at just this location and look exactly like hands at a spot where hands would naturally be expected to be found? I would call that even less likely than seeing a ghost!

There is a ghost near the Prison Field. Whose is it? This we will try to determine next.

CHAPTER NINE: IDENTIFYING THE GHOST

Who was the singing ghost of the Old Joliet prison? Because the singing originated somewhere in the Prison's Field almost everyone automatically assumes that the ghost must have belonged to a convict. This is not necessarily true.

There are many reasons why a ghost might haunt a location. One reason is because it died there or lived a large part of its life in that location and has chosen to return to it for one reason or another.

It is important to account for the reason why the haunting started on July 15th if possible. A recent burial in the potter's field, irrespective of cause of death, would have been the most likely cause of the start of the sudden haunting. Having checked the records of execution and of burials in the potter's field for the period of early July 1932, nothing was found for either of these events having occurred. Thus, a recent burial or execution wasn't the cause.

The next cause for a haunting might be to commemorate the day that a person died – the anniversary of that date. It is very common for a ghost to make an appearance on the anniversary of its death at a location that was significant to the spirit, not necessarily the location of its death. One ghost in Florida would appear outside her bedroom window on each anniversary of her death because she loved that area so much in life.

A search for a death anniversary in the matter of the singing ghost proved successful for not one but three people. Three convicts from the Old Prison had been hanged on July 15, 1927 at the Will County Jail which is not far from the prison. All three had once been prisoners at the Old Prison.

On May 5, 1925 Deputy Warden Peter N. Klein was stabbed and beaten to death in his office by a group of prison inmates. The seven inmates had requested a meeting with the deputy warden and were granted the privilege. However, no sooner had they entered his office than he was brutally set upon, being stabbed with knives, scissors and beaten by an iron bar. Taking a guard and a trustee hostage, the murderers then fled the office. The two hostages were later released unharmed, but they were left tied to a tree.

Five days later five of the seven killers were captured but a police officer and a member of the sheriff's posse were shot and wounded during the capture. The other two men were captured four months later on November 26th.

The seven men were put on trial and six of them were found guilty of murder and sentenced to be hung by the neck until dead. The six convicts were placed in Will County Jail in Joliet. But on March 27, 1927 the six convicts made an escape attempt with the help of one of the guards. Three of the convicts were immediately apprehended, but the other three got away. They forced their way into a cab and made the driver take them to the south side of Chicago, which is where almost all escapees from Joliet flee.

Alerted of the escape from Will County Jail, three Chicago police officers – of one of the best forces in the country – gave chase to the cab and stopped it. A gun battle ensued. Chicago Police Officer Leo Grant was shot and killed while another officer and the cab driver were seriously wounded.

One of the escapees was shot and killed, one was taken into custody and the third escaped. The third man was eventually captured. In all, three of the original seven faced execution by hanging, the other two having been killed in their escape attempts, and a third, Bernardo Roa, had escaped to Mexico and would elude the gallows.

The three men who might be candidates for the singing ghost are: Charlie Duschowski, Robert Torrez, and Walter Stalesky. Not only did their violent deaths by hanging occur on July 15th five years before the singing ghost made itself known but these were people of strong-willed, single-minded personalities which are usually the types who come back to haunt.

However, these three men were vicious, cold blooded murderers. None of the three seemed the type to sing church hymns in Latin or announce their appearance by singing anything. Just because they are dead does not mean that they have been reformed.

It is important to note again that the singing of the ghost only SOUNDED LIKE Latin hymns and that no one really could understand the words.

Is it possible that more than one ghost haunts the Prison Field and only one of them does the singing? After all, the potter's field is full of lost souls. But, again, why did the singing begin when it did? Any one of the persons buried here could have a particular date to commemorate by reappearing on this plane of existence.

And let's not forget the spirit of the murdered warden. Could it be his ghost that appeared in the fields just outside of his former office?

There are two other types of people who might be candidates for the ghost, although a specific person cannot be pinpointed. Ironically, one of these two potential ghosts could be associated with the quarry on the prison property. No, not the trustee convict, but some unknown swimmer who'd drowned in the quarry.

After heavy rains or when the quarry had not been pumped out for a lengthy period there would be a great deal of water buildup here and the local children would see this as a chance to go for a swim. There are several quarries in the Joliet area and unfortunately death by drowning in them was a very common occurrence. It's possible that one of the drowning victims in the prison quarry went on to haunt the surroundings.

Another possibility is that the ghost was a fisherman. Why? Because of the question that the ghost put to the fisherman whom he met hurrying home through the Prison Field. Who but a fellow fisherman would be so concerned about another fisherman's catch that day? And people used to fish in the Prison Field.

There is another story of sudden, brutal murder associated with the Old Joliet Prison which could possibly offer a clue to the ghost's identity. It involves the murder of a warden's wife who happened to be renowned for her great talent as a singer.

CHAPTER TEN – ANGEL OF JOLIET

Odette Maizee Bordeaux Allen was known as the angel of Joliet because of her enchanting singing ability. She sang like an angel – or, possibly a ghost?

Odette was famous for her performances on the stage in New Orleans but gave this up to marry the warden of the old Joliet Prison, Edmund "Ned" Allen who was a widower with two small children. The nationally respected warden had been speaking at a conference on penology in New Orleans when he met his wife-to-be.

On June 19, 1915 the warden finished the conference and traveled directly to Chicago to meet with politicians concerning building the new Statesville Prison on the outskirts of Joliet. Before meeting with the politicians, however, Warden Allen had stopped off at a jeweler to buy an expensive diamond ring that he was going to give to his wife at dinner that evening.

But there was a problem. Odette's dressmaker wasn't able to complete the dress she'd planned on wearing at the dinner she was going to attend with her husband in Chicago. So she contacted him and told him she would remain in Joliet.

Odette spent the evening with her two step-children at a movie theatre in downtown Joliet. With a convict acting as chauffeur, Odette and the children were returned to the warden's house inside the prison at about 10:45 p.m.

All of the servants in the warden's house were convicts, some of them convicted murderers. Among them was a notorious 29 year-old convicted murderer Joe Campbell, better known as "Chicken Joe." For some reason, Odette had called on him to serve her personally in the early morning of June 15, 1915.

At 6 a.m. Joe was asked to fill the woman's water container on the nightstand, get her some coffee and bring in the morning newspaper. After he'd done all of this, he was dismissed until he would be needed again at 9:00 a.m.

What happened next isn't known. But at 6:30 a.m. smoke began to pour out of the warden's home. Guards raced to the building, rushed up the stairs to Odette's second floor bedroom from where the smoke was coming. The door was locked. They broke it down and helped the firefighters put out the blaze which was mostly centered on the woman's bed.

Odette was still in bed, scorched beyond recognition. It was later determined that she'd had her skull fractured and had most likely been sexually assaulted.

There were three convicts who were attending Odette that morning, including "Chicken Joe" and all three of them were placed in isolation after the woman's murder.

Odette was buried in Oakwood Cemetery – one of Joliet's most prominent – and most of the city was shut down that day for the funeral.

"Chicken Joe" claimed his innocence but he was put on trial for the murder anyway, even though there were two other suspects who could have been just as guilty. Even though there wasn't any real proof against Joseph Campbell he was convicted on circumstantial evidence and was sentenced to be hung.

But the governor of Illinois, E. F. Dunne, thought that the conviction was unfair. He commuted Joe's sentence to life in prison and that's where Campbell died in 1950 at the age of 64.

Is it possible that the singing ghost is Odette? Even though the voice had been described as a baritone one other person thought it sounded more like a banshee.

However, the ghost actually spoke to at least one person – the fisherman – and, although he didn't mention the gender of the spirit, it could be assumed that it was male.

Although Odette and the others already mentioned had the potential to be ghosts in this case of haunting, it is much more likely that the spirit may belong to an entirely different century. This will become clear by examining a different part of the photograph of the ghost, involving an article of clothing.

CHAPTER ELEVEN – FRENCH INFLUENCE

From 1717 to 1763 the French had a large stake in America and this is a very important part of this story. Louis Joliet and Father Jacques Marquette were the first White Men to travel the Mississippi River and visit what was to become Illinois. Since that time there has been French influence in this region, particularly Joliet which the two famous explorers visited in 1673. Louis Joliet's statue is below.

The French first came to this area to conduct trapping and fur trading. The eastern part of the continent was already suffering from deforestation so the fur traders went ever westward. And fur trading was a very big business, one which the native population did not get involved in.

The French built several forts in Illinois to secure their possessions. Fort de Chartres was constructed in the southern part of the state and acted as the seat of French government. Fort Creve Coeur was built near modern day Peoria and Fort St. Louis was built on the Illinois River about fifty miles west of the Joliet area (but was quickly abandoned). The Prison Field would have been at that time much like it was in 1932. It would have been good land both for farming, raising cattle and trapping. There was also water available.

In 1752 Illinois was dominated by the French, even though the population consisted only of 284 men, 132 women and 352 children. There also was a large force of about 300 soldiers stationed at Fort de Chartres.

The French lost all of their Illinois possessions when they were defeated in the French and Indian War. It is important to note that the French people who were living in Illinois chose to relocate to Spanish held land on the continent rather than stay under British rule because the Spanish shared their Catholic religion. Religion was of extreme importance to the people of this period.

What does any of this have to do with the singing ghost? This information may be vital in establishing the ghost's identity.

A closer examination of the photograph of the ghost will be needed. Notice the head area of the ghost in the photograph below. There is obviously something on his head.

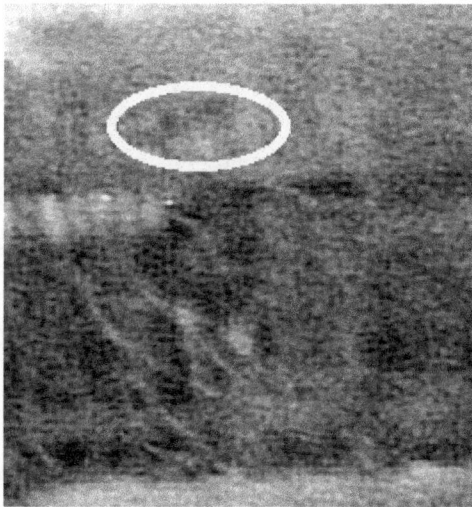

He appears to be wearing a hat. The type of hat looks like what a cocked hat, otherwise known as a three corned hat, would look like from a distance. Compare the ghost's head gear with that which was worn by a French military man of the eighteenth century.

Note the tip of the soldier's hat where the two front sides are drawn together into a beak. The same type of beak seems to exist in the ghost's cap, distinguished by a tiny area of white (straight line points toward it).

While the ghost in the photograph may be wearing a cocked hat it is more likely the ghost is wearing the type of hat pictured below which is the type worn by French infantry during the French and Indian War.

This should help in identifying him at least by time frame. An additional identifier is the long black coat the ghost is wearing. This was also worn by the French during the time of the French and Indian War. It's clear that the clothing worn by the spirit is crucial at least in pinpointing the era from which he'd come back to haunt.

Note in the photo below how the collars of the coat extend quite high and up along where the cheeks would be. Then compare that to the side of the face of the ghost which seems to be enclosed in some form of material.

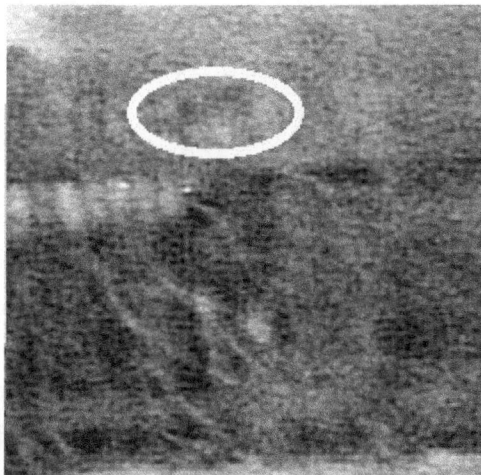

It seems highly likely that the ghost belongs to a French soldier or a local militiaman who was living in this part of the country sometime between 1750 and 1763. Imagine being so far from home and fighting in a war that probably didn't mean that very much to him. Perhaps this was a lonely soldier who would cheer himself up by singing.

The ghost's singing in a foreign language is the reason why he would more likely belong to a French soldier rather than a British or Colonial soldier. Those people who heard the singing ghost in 1932 were all agreed on one point: the words were in a language other than English. If the soldier sang in French – being a romance language related to Latin – it could sound very much like church hymns he was singing. Or, being French he was probably a Roman Catholic and would possibly know certain hymns in Latin.

But what would cause his ghost to become active on July 15, 1932? This is a question more difficult to answer. Perhaps it was a significant date in the life of the ghost. It could have been anything that the spirit wanted to commemorate. Perhaps, being a ghost he had insight into the future and was celebrating the French Revolution which historically began on July 14. A ghost could be a day early, couldn't he?

Below is a picture of what a French soldier would look like during the time of the French and Indian War.

They look very similar, do they not?

The ghost does have a face. All of the features can be plainly seen. However, the face isn't large enough or detailed enough to define any better. Additional magnification simply destroys the features that do exist.

The impression given is that this is the face of a very young man, possibly about 18 years old. He looks to be a sad young soldier in a strange land.

But look more closely to his right. Are there two additional faces on his right side, two more soldiers? Their bodies aren't visible but a pair of faces appear to be next to the ghost's. Look more closely at that part of the picture.

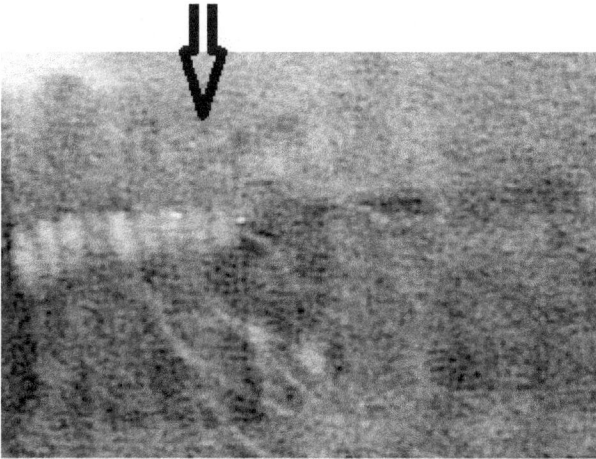

It is probable that instead of a convict singing from the depths of a quarry the true voice of the singing ghost belongs to the spirit of a French soldier from the early days of the colonization of Illinois by France.

There is another possibility to be considered. At the time, France was a devoutly Catholic country and had a great many priests and missionaries in America who were trying to convert the native population. Jesuits were in the forefront of the battle for the Red Man's souls. In the Catholic cause, Jesuits are like the shock troops or the marines of their religion. They volunteer for the most dangerous missions. They are also the highest educated among the Catholic ranks with a great many scientific discoveries having been made by Jesuits.

It wouldn't be unlikely that a Jesuit missionary had ventured into the region that is the present day Prison Field to convert the native population living there. The ghost may belong to one of the missionaries. He would certainly be skilled at singing church hymns in Latin!

The French influence in Illinois was extensive at this time. It was the linchpin between Canada and New Orleans with the Mississippi, the Illinois, the Des Plains and the Fox Rivers providing a perfect water route from the deep South to the high North.

But we now have possession of a picture of the ghost. It's difficult to deny that it looks like a young person. And the position of the hands suggests that he might be a young person in peril, trying to fend off an attack. Despite all of the other possibilities, it seems likely that the ghost is that of a youthful French soldier serving his country in a far off land.

A person may or may not agree with this conclusion. But the photograph proves one thing: there was a real ghost(s) in Joliet's Prison Field!

CHAPTER TWELVE – OTHER OBSERVATIONS

In the early 1960's, about thirty years after the incident of the singing ghost, when I was still very young I was shocked one early evening to hear the sound of singing coming from the top of the Prison Field's hill, from where the potter's field was located. At the time, I was standing on Woodruff Road and as such I was at the very edge of the Prison Field and almost a mile from the source of the sound. The singing was real. It was loud. It was almost as if it was coming from directly in front of me. But I couldn't decipher any of the words.

Was this a reprise of the singing ghost? To find out, I raced home to ask my mother. She would know. She heard the original singing ghost.

When I got home and told my mother about the singing she stepped out onto the porch to listen. Our house was much closer to the source of the sound than Woodruff Road and the singing was even louder here. Unfortunately, my mother shook her head and replied, "No, it's only the Holy Rollers singing from a church on top of the hill." By the way, the term "Holy Roller" is here used with respect for a people infused with the spirit of the Holy Ghost.

My hopes were crushed. So, I decided to locate this church on the hill, even though it was nighttime. I could find my way through the hills and woods in the dark that is how intimately I knew the entire area.

However, I couldn't find the church on the hill that night. What I located was an old boarded up building that used to be a church. Was I hearing ghostly singing from a haunted church?

Ironically, this church would have been right in the middle of "The Hill" subdivision if the church had been in existence in 1932. Imagine what that would have done to the singing ghost story? Would they have been considered competing ghosts?

My experience with hearing the "Holy Rollers" singing from so far away demonstrated the immense conductive power of sound in this region. I may not have heard the singing ghost, but after hearing the "holy rollers" I could easily understand how such a sound could be heard clearly anywhere within the confines of the Prison Field, including the hilltop and surrounding neighborhoods.

It would be as if you could clearly hear the voices of people speaking on a street corner seven blocks away from your front porch or driveway.

Even though the hoax theory has been completely discredited, a person might be tempted to think that since the powers of sound transmission are so strong in this location it might have been possible for someone singing in the quarry to transmit a voice over long distances. But it isn't. Not from that location. And that's been one of the problems with that explanation for the singing ghost all along. The sound simply could not have come from the quarry.

A voice could not escape from the depths of the quarry and then float freely across the countryside. Several experts in sound have already testified to this. The limestone walls of the quarry trap sound.

In the Prison Field environment, the conductive powers of sound carry it in only one direction – down into the lower lying plain or field. This was made very clear when I heard the singing from the "Holy Roller" church. Sound does not go upward in reverse here. Neither does it travel upward from the depths of the quarry.

This was the last possible argument to be waged in favor of any possibility about a hoax from the quarry – the amazing conductive powers of sound of the Prison

Field. But the sounds only come from above, not below. And, in a very real sense, that is the direction from which the voice of the singing ghost was coming.

APPENDIX A

NOTE: what follows are copies of the actual newspaper reports about the singing ghost. These are not reprints or modernized versions but the genuine articles from the *Joliet Evening-Herald* of 1932. Begin with Article one.

GHOST THRILLS
HUNDREDS AT
POTTERS' FIELD

Crowds Wait All Night for
Eerie Song at Graves of
Convicts.

SONGS IN LATIN

Out of the gloom of Potter's field on "Monkey Hill", back of the women's old prison on Collins street, a singing spectre arises nightly to roar Latin liturgies thru an awed silence held by 600 thrill-seekers huddled on graves about him.

So state many who say they have heard the mournful, monotonous intonations without seeing the singer.

The midnight torch-singer made his first spirit appearance on the Saturday night, July 14, those who claim to have heard the voice say, when the full moon first crossed the fair sky.

Rumors of the spirit singing were started by householders living immediately east of the Woodruff road at the top of the hill south of Collins street, which over-looks the rear of the women's state penitentiary in the distance. They claim they heard an awful wailing coming from the Potter's field back of their homes on that first night at 11:45 o'clock.

Bad Men Buried There.

In that field are buried the unclaimed bodies of dead convicts who died at the penitentiary up to a few years ago. The field has not been used in recent years. In that field, residents of the locality recall, are the bodies of men who have cause to lie uneasy in their graves. Murderers lie there, and kidnapers, ... and villainous rogues of all

and villainous rogues of all…

kinds.

"Right here under us", bolder persons torment more timid youths as they sit on the mounds each night awaiting the Latin hymns to throw a chill thru the throngs.

Word of the midnight singing spread rapidly thru the north end and to Lockport. Hundreds now gather nightly into safe, compact groups on the cemetery lots.

600 at Scene Last Night.

Six hundred persons visited the scene last night, coming after 9 o'clock and many staying thru the night. Automobiles streamed up Woodruff road at 11 o'clock in a steady lane. Parking facilities were offered in a field near the cemetery, and boys directed traffic without charge.

In the cemetery youths and adults stumble over sunken graves and trip over head-stones in the dark. Shouting and cat-calling echo from group to group. Bold youths form patrols and, with torchlights and lanterns, inspect every square foot of the cemetery, looking for hidden wires which may prove the Singing Spectre a hoax. But in ten nights, now, none have been found.

As midnight approaches silence settles down, and many lights are dimmed. Only low conversation is heard, where before all was hubbub. Midnight is the hour when all union hour ghosts do their stuff, it is remembered.

Many Heard It.

Story-tellers collect groups and thrill their listeners with ghost stories, and, perhaps, even recall experiences of their own with ghosts. Others stimulate themselves with the thought that they are no such things.

"But this one is real", a voice says out of the darkness, "I heard it myself last night—"

"So did I, it was only five feet behind me—"

All agree that no one has ever seen the "Monkey Hill" ghost; a voice singing in Latin verse is heard, loud and vibrant rising out of the hollow night, and that is all. If left alone, the voice goes on several minutes, but daring boys with lanterns usually ferret out the spot and the singing stops.

None of those who heard the voice recognize the Latin songs. They are not of a cheerful nature, it is agreed, but rather express the distressed thoughts of a tormented soul.

Ghost Demands Quiet.

Last night midnight came and went with no spirit singing. The ghost sings only when the crowd is quiet and still, the "regulars" claim. The first night it gave its eerie call at 11:45 o'clock, and one night it sang at midnight sharp, but it is usually later than that. The crowd, in the majority, is content to sit and wait. Sunday night the Latin songs came from nowhere at 4 o'clock in the morning.

Those who stayed up that late say they heard the singing at 3 o'clock this morning, after the rowdy, unbelieving persons had left for home.

"The ghost is self-conscious", the believers say, "and doesn't like to be laughed at. It's a good ghost and

at least it hasn't hurt anyone, at least not yet. (End of first article)

89

SECOND ARTICLE:

SINGING GHOST FAILS TO APPEAR BEFORE 3000

"Too Much Noise and Excitement," Say Those Who Have Heard It.

THRONGS WAIT

Retiring in the face of superior odds, the Singing Spectre moped in his convict's grave in Potter's field on "Monkey Hill" last night when 3,000 noisy persons appeared to hear the Latin song he has sung, it is said, for ten successive nights.

At 4 o'clock this morning, when a diffused light paled the eastern sky and dispelled the hopes of 200 remaining ghost hunters, the spirit bard still grieved in sullen silence.

"He doesn't like crowds," those familiar with the ghost declared. "It has made him obstinate to see these people stomping about the graves and disturbing his thoughts and the thoughts of his mates."

And crowds there were. At 10 o'clock hundreds of automobiles began turning off Collins street at the women's old penitentiary and heading up the Woodruff road in a continuous stream. Cars came from all parts of Joliet, from Lockport and Rockdale, Plainfield, Aurora, Chicago Heights and other county centers. Chicago was also represented.

Midnight and No Ghost.

...was like a New...

Year's Eve party. Men looked at their watches and shouted the time as midnight approached;

"A quarter to 12—"

"Five minutes to go—"

Automobile head lights, spot-lights on swivels, hand flash-lights swept the plat for rods around and beaconed the sky.

"It is now two minutes to 12 o'clock...."

"12 o'clock."

Midnight passed but the Singing Spectre had lost his tongue.

The ghost hunters settled down to "see it thru." Tiny camp fires were lit. Old thrillers were re-told to fear tingling listeners, and old legends uncovered:

"Sure, and it may be the banshee crying," an Irish ancient offered. "Back in the days when I lived in the auld country, I heard her often. She crys steadily, night after night, when some good soul dies on earth. Perhaps her Gaelic has been mistaken for Latin. She is a little old woman, and always combing and brushing her streaming gray hair as she cries."

Some Sleep, Others Sing.

Men curled up in blankets and slept fitfully, on haunted ground. Others formed quartets, quintets and larger groups to chorus old songs together. "Deep River" rolled over the graves, and lighter numbers followed. Coffee was drunk from thermos jugs as the sky turned to an inverted pewter saucer and a damp wind swelled.

Hours started to pass, and many thrill seekers left for home. Others gradually lost faith in the ghost. "No one ever heard a voice. It's all a figment, a product of the heat."

Tells of Hearing Voice.

Those who believed in the "voice" knew the presence of hundreds of persons would stop the show, and went to their homes in glum silence. Among these was Stanley Dudek, 21 years old, Juniper avenue. The back yard of his home breaks on the Potter's field fence.

"My mother heard the singing first of all," he said last night. "She was in the house with my sister, Genevieve, the Saturday before last and heard the singing about 11:30 o'clock. They went out in the back to see who was singing, and turned flashlights on the spot, but could see no one. My father, George Dudek, and I were out that night, but heard the singing the next and went out in the cemetery to investigate. We found nothing. Other neighbors have also heard the voice.

"We heard it every night until the crowds started to bother the 'thing.' It has a sweet voice, but very strong, altho words can never be distinguished. We think it sings in Latin. Starting with low, hideous gurgling sounds, the song breaks suddenly strong and reaches very high notes. But it is a beautiful singer. If they catch the one doing the singing they ought to put him on the stage, ghost or not."

Residents Disturbed.

Dudek said residents in the region at first stayed out of the cemetery and the song continued for long periods. "It stops when men go after it, tho," he added.

Those living in homes near the cemetery are growing disturbed as the crowds grow larger and stay later, and are considering a complaint to authorities. Besides giving them peace, that move would offer a better chance to unearth the ghost, they believe, as he is bolder when his audience is small.

Fisherman Heard Him.

The spirit does not always sing or chant, according to some of those who have heard him. One of the first to encounter the "hant" was a fisherman residing in Forest Park who was cutting across the prison field about two weeks ago. It was night, but the moon lighted the

(Continued on Page Two).

92

countryside, making visible the
lumpy mounds on "Monkey Hill" that
are the graves.

"Any luck tonight?" the fisherman
heard someone ask.

He looked around for the voice
which seemed to come from behind
but there was no one there.

At first, the fisherman said, he believed it was Graham McNamee, yet
the voice tone and inflection were
different. He was a polite man, this
angler, and he was somewhat puzzled
at hearing voices yet not seeing a
speaker. He explained that he did not
answer because he lost the use of
his speech momentarily thru surprise.

"I had little if any luck, fishing,"
the man went on, "and if I don't
have any better running than I did
fishing I don't know what I'm going to do."

But his legs remained faithful and
the angler tore off across the cemetery, fairly skimming the ground. It
is said that he stepped in a hole and
fell near the road, but his momentum
was so great that he was able to roll
the next hundred yards.

It is expected that another crowd
will keep vigil tonight and perhaps
they may be rewarded.

THIRD ARTICLE

FIND GHOST IS ONLY CONVICT SINGING AT WORK

Trusty Who Inspected Pumps in Quarry Croons Ballads During Night.

SOME UNCONVINCED

The Singing Spectre of Potter's field on "Monkey Hill" is only an Irish-German prison trusty singing in jubilation as he awaits a parole scheduled to come within two weeks, William Lalon Chrysler, the singer, told in a full confession to Warden E. M. Stubblefield of the old prison this afternoon.

Chrysler was detailed three weeks ago as a night-watchman at the prison quarry and property back of the women's old penitentiary on North Collins street near the Potter's field. His voice is noted thruout the penitentiary for its rich qualities, and Chrysler is by nature a happy type who sings at his work.

Awaits Parole.

Two weeks ago he was notified that he is to be paroled within a month. While tending his midnight duties on the plain beneath Monkey Hill, Chrysler has made a habit of singing. It was not until last week that a guard told him his singing was taking on ghostly proportions. After that, Chrysler, in good humor, lifted a few lusty bars and watched the effect on the crowds at the cemetery above him. When patrols searched out the voice, Chrysler hid behind a bush in the shadows, he told Warden

94

Stubblefield this afternoon.

Sentenced from Cook county for larceny, Chrysler came to the penitentiary on a one to ten year count for larceny. Chrysler has served four years of the term. He is 33 years old. His father was German and his mother Irish.

"I don't know any foreign language, and did all the singing in English," he told Warden Stubblefield at this afternoon's ghost quiz. "A guard told me the "ghost" was supposed to sing in Latin, so occasionally I mumbled some words to church tunes which I remembered."

A loose tongue effected the unshrouding. Chrysler, a trusty, assigned the task three weeks ago of inspecting pumps in the quarry thrice a night, bragged to fellow convicts yesterday of his ghostly talents. Thousands were attracted this week to hear the songs, which seemed to burst from the mounds of dead convicts under the feet of the listeners.

A Rich Baritone Voice.

Chrysler's story spread thru the penitentiary and reached authorities. Warden Frank C. Whipp last night had a second trustee detailed to listen in on Chrysler's singing. The shadow's report to the warden today carried the conviction that the Lithuanian tunes raised by Chrysler in the prison quarry, more than a quarter of a mile distant from Potter's field, were the same which were believed by thrill-seekers to be Latin hymns sung by a baritone ghost.

Chrysler, a veteran convict, is known thruout the penitentiary for his voice, a rich, vibrant baritone. He habitually sings at his work, specializing in Lithuanian folk songs learned in his youth. He was placed on the quarry duty three week. ago and has since inspected the pumps three times a week.

Quarry a Sounding Board.

Splendid sounding boards are offered by the bare rock walls of the quarry, and, with the aid of a north wind, the songs are distinctly carried to the prison cemetery where the throngs gather. Ventriloquism, thought by many to be the secret of the ghost, is unknown to Chrysler.

96

and, according to statements of magicians and stage ventriloquists, could not be practiced over such a large distance at night. The art depends upon attracting the attention of listeners to a definite spot; the voice heard at Potter's field was said to appear at different points on different nights.

Last night and the night before, when thousands were disappointed when the "ghost" failed to sing, the wind was from the east and adverse to Chrysler's singing.

Chrysler sang at first for his own pleasure and to relieve the lonesome monotony of his rounds. It was not until late last week that he discovered the consternation his songs were arousing. The humor of the situation struck his fancy and he continued his folk ballads with zeal.

Diminished Crowd.

A slightly diminished crowd visited Potter's field last night to await the "ghost singing," which failed to develop because the wind was wrong. Early in the night they arrived at the site, but only a few hundred remained at 12:30 o'clock. Interest in the "ghost" waned when the singing was not heard Tuesday night.

A delegate from Sickle Center, Missouri, camped on the grounds last night. "Folks in my town read of this Singing Spectre in the newspapers but they won't believe it until they hear from me," the delegate, Joshua Jones, said, "and you have to show me."

Belief Still Persists.

Belief in the Singing Spectre still exists, however, by residents of the Monkey Hill district who heard the singing before the crowds gathered from the county.

No man can sing loud enough to be heard from the prison quarry to beyond Potter's field, is their opinion,

(Continued on Page Two),

During Vacation

FIND GHOST IS
ONLY CONVICT
SINGING AT WORK

(Continued from Page One)

and no man can sing such unearthly songs. Pinning the thing on Chrysler is just a scheme of prison officials, grown nervous, to disperse the crowds in the region, they declare.

"It is hard to believe," Stanley Dudek, Juniper avenue, a youth who was among the first to hear the singing, said last night, "that that gurgling take-off of the singer is only the starting of a pump in the prison quarry."

A commercial "racket" took seed at Potter's field last night when a group of boys established parking rates and demanded payment under threat of breaking windshields, according to a report received at the sheriff's office. The complaining men declared the boys asked 15 cents when the automobiles were parked, and another 15 cents when the machines left the area.

"If you don't pay up, we'll smash your windshield", the boys are reported to have threatened.

Have you noticed the various inconsistencies in the above series of articles? One of the most important is the various identities ascribed to Mr. Chrysler. He is said to be of German-Irish background yet he sings hymns in the Lithuanian language that he'd learned while a youth. Why would an Irish-German child be taught Lithuanian by his parents? These types of factual distortions are things to particularly notice.

In the same article, the convict Chrysler is said to have been interviewed by Warden Stubblefield and Warden Fred C. Whipp. So which man was the real warden?

There is constant confusion between the insultingly named "Monkey Hill" and Potter's field throughout the series of articles. Obviously, the reporter himself didn't know the difference.

APPENDIX B

France in Illinois

Louis Joliet and Father Marquette made the existence of the empire of France possible in North America. They did this by their exploration of the Mississippi River, the Illinois River, the Des Plains River and the Fox River. This placed Illinois firmly in the center of New France and joined Canada with New Orleans which also joined the Atlantic Ocean with the Gulf of Mexico.

Illinois is a French reworking of the Native American word Illini a word which meant something similar to "superior people."

Louis Joliet was born in Quebec on September 21, 1645. His father was a wagon-maker. Joliet received minor orders in the Catholic Church (less than the priesthood) and gave up his studies in theology to become an explorer. With the vast experience he acquired, he was the man for the tough job of exploring down the "great river" and opening up the land of Illinois to the French.

Although the French had hoped to colonize America as had the British they quickly learned that for them it wasn't economically feasible. There wasn't any vast wealth in trapping and the only types of mines in the areas they possessed were lead and copper which at that time were not great moneymakers.

One of the major reasons the French fought the British was to keep them from encroaching on French land by crossing the Appalachian Mountains. What was later to become the Seven Years War between Britain and France had its beginnings with the fighting in North America which began in 1754. The British formally declared war on France in 1756.

Illinois was sparsely populated by the French. But there were numerous small communities spread widely throughout the state.

An example of a typical French building in America.

French influence ended with the completion of the French and Indian War. France lost most of its territory in North America, although some of its residents may have remained in the form of ghosts.

APPENDIX C

A similar ghost story

There is another ghost story which is somewhat similar to that of the singing ghost in that it involved thousands of witnesses and the event occurred repeatedly at regular times.

The story was printed in the *Philadelphia Press, March 25, 1884.* It is reprinted here verbatim.

DAYTON, O., March 25. — A thousand people surround the grave yard in Miamisburg, a town near here, every night to witness the antics of what appears to be a genuine ghost. There is no doubt about the existence of the apparition, as Mayor Marshall, the revenue collector and hundreds of prominent citizens all testify to having seen it. Last night several hundred people, armed with clubs and guns, assaulted the specter, which appeared to be a woman in white. Clubs, bullets and shot tore the air in which the mystic figure floated without disconcerting it in the least. A portion of the town turned out en masse to-day and began exhuming all the bodies in the cemetery.

The remains of the Buss family, composed of three people, have already been exhumed. The town is visited daily by hundreds of strangers and none are disappointed, as the apparition is always on duty promptly at 9 o'clock. The strange figure was at once recognized by the inhabitants of the town as a young lady supposed to have been murdered several years ago. Her attitude while drifting among the graves is one of deep thought, with the head inclined forward and hands clasped behind.

THE END